My Magical Words

The Magic of Me Series

ISBN: 978-1-7325963-4-4 (hardcover)
ISBN: 978-1-7325963-5-1 (ebook)

Library of Congress Control Number: 2019900568

Illustrations by Zuzana Svobodová
Book design by Zuzana Svobodová, Maškrtáreň
Editing by Laura Boffa

First printing edition 2019.

Boundless Movement

Visit www.authorbcummings.com

THE MAGIC OF ME
MY MAGICAL WORDS

WRITTEN BY
BECKY CUMMINGS

ILLUSTRATED BY
ZUZANA SVOBODOVÁ

DEDICATION

To my three magical children,
Tyson, Calvin, and Faith.
May the world become brighter
because of you. Believe in your magic!

THIS BOOK BELONGS TO:

TIPS FOR READING WITH CHILDREN

- Have children repeat the positive affirmations after you.

- Create an action to go with each positive affirmation. For example, have children flex their muscles when they say, "I am strong!"

- Ask children to give other examples that show the positive affirmation. For example, after reading the page about kindness you could ask, "What are other ways you show that you are kind?"

The words you speak have super powers!

They can bring sunshine or rain showers.

So here are some magical things you can say,

to bring the sun and light up your day!

Listen closely to this life advice.

Start with, 'I am' and end with something nice!

The more you say these words, the more they come true.

So, repeat them quite often, because

THE MAGIC'S IN YOU!

I am special!

You are a masterpiece, one-of-a kind,

created perfectly with an eye for design.

From your hair, to your toes, to the way that you speak,

all of these differences make you UNIQUE!

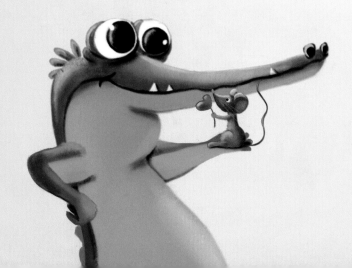

I am giving!

You share what is yours and make someone's day,

and give others a turn so more people can play!

When you give you don't ask for something back.

You care that others have enough, not that you lack.

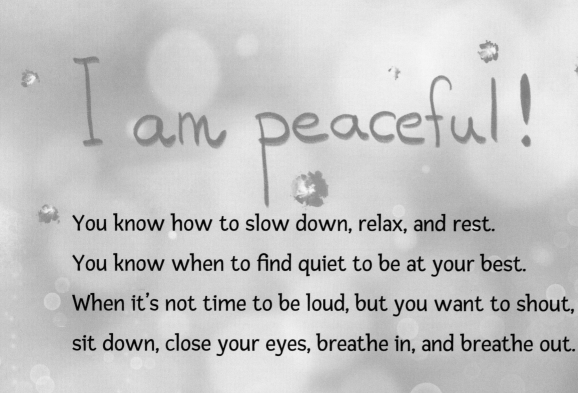

I am peaceful!

You know how to slow down, relax, and rest.

You know when to find quiet to be at your best.

When it's not time to be loud, but you want to shout,

sit down, close your eyes, breathe in, and breathe out.

I am kind!

You use your voice to say nice words.

You lift people up like wind under birds.

You don't use your words to offend or tease.

You give compliments, you say

THANKS and PLEASE!

I am loved !

Just by being yourself, you fill people with joy.

You are a special girl or boy!

People love you for the many things you have to share.

You are surrounded by people who care!

I am smart!

You listen and learn from the people you love.

Sometimes you look within or above.

It's fun to learn all of the things YOU CAN DO.

Then you are able to TEACH OTHERS TOO!

I am strong!

You run, you jump, you play all day.

Your bones and muscles shout, "HOORAY!"

They love the daily exercise.

It makes them want to

DOUBLE IN SIZE!

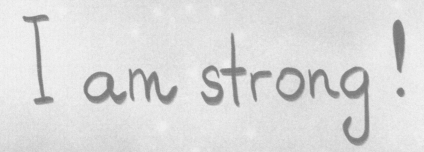

I am healthy!

You eat vegetables and fruits galore.

You drink your water, but wait, there's more!

Even though sweet treats might taste YUMMY,

you don't eat too many because they're bad for your TUMMY.

I am thankful!

You are grateful for what fills each day,

like the people you love and places you stay!

With gifts that you get and the fun things you do,

you always remember to say,

"THANK YOU!"

I am happy!

You laugh so hard your belly shakes.

You smile so wide that your cheeks ache.

You lift others up when they feel down,

by spreading your

JOY ALL AROUND!

I am proud of myself !

You always try to give your best.

When you work hard, you pass the test.

You can do it... You did it! HIP-HIP-HOORAY!

You try new things and learn every day.

I am beautiful!

Inside and outside your beauty shines bright.

You glow with love like the moon in the night.

True beauty comes from your heart deep inside.

It sneaks out and pops up, on your smile so wide.

You can be anything you believe.

So say, "I AM" and be ready to receive.

May all your precious dreams come true,

now that you know

THE MAGIC IS IN YOU!

SPECIAL AS CAN BE

THIS IS THE
MAGIC OF ME!

YOUR PICTURE HERE!

Dear Readers,

Thank you for reading *My Magical Words* to your child or children. I hope every time they hear this book, the words make them feel incredible and inspire them to live healthy and happy lives.

If you feel *My Magical Words* should be shared with others, the best way to help it reach more children is to leave an honest review on Amazon and share it on social media. Your words and photos will help others learn about my book and encourage me to keep on writing!

If you enjoyed this book, be sure to check out my other books.

Your support is a blessing. Thank you!

With love,

Becky

#themagicofme
#authorbcummings

Becky Cummings is an author, teacher and mom of three. She loves kids and speaking her truth. Becky is blessed to combine these passions by writing children's books that spread messages of love, hope, faith, health, and happiness. When she isn't writing, you might find her salsa dancing, eating a veggie burrito at her favorite Mexican joint, or traveling to new places! Becky is available for author visits and wants to connect with you so be sure to visit her on Facebook fb.me/authorbcummings, or Instagram and visit her website, www.authorbcummings.com.

Zuzana Svobodová is an illustrator. She uses both digital and traditional techniques, as well as the world of fantasy delivered happily by her two children to bring stories to life. When she isn't working on illustrations, she enjoys drawing, doing and teaching yoga, dreaming and baking sweets.